Otter

ENCOUNTERS IN THE WILD

JIM CRUMLEY

Saraband

ONE

THE TIDE IS ON THE RISE. The fragment of the Atlantic Ocean that crams itself into the Sound of Sleat is a troublesome cross-hatching of currents, at once furrowed and swirled, placid and frantic. Only the shoreline rocks and the otter-watcher perched there are still.

Every hour that you can be still on a Skye shore is repaid by diverse wonders. Let only your eyes wander. Have them roam the shores and that sliver of ocean surging by. Because in time, in time, something will happen.

And in time, the otter happens. It is a little to the south, a hundred yards away and fifty yards out into the Sound. But if you have been still enough for long enough, your eyes will have attuned and

1

begun to read the sea-surge fluently, so you recognise the blunt curve and flourished tail of a diving otter for what it is. Home your eyes in on that portion of the sea, permit nothing else to move, and you will see the otter resurface. Perhaps that is the moment when you notice for the first time that in the diving, the underwatering, the eel-catching and the resurfacing, the otter has advanced twenty yards north against the current. So it is coming closer.

The eel is devoured on the surface, held between the otter's front paws, dying bit by bit from the head downwards. It's what some otters do so that they might live, and it's how some eels die.

Then the whole cycle of events happens again. There is another blunt curve (the tail a raised exclamation mark), another dive, another eel snared, and in the process the otter has advanced another twenty northbound yards up the Sound. So not only is it coming closer, but there is also a rhythm to its progress.

Now, look around you while it is underwater. You are looking for a certain kind of offshore rock, and if you are ready to move the next time the otter dives, you can make it as far as that little onshore outcrop over there. Why there? Because then you will be no more than thirty yards from a flat offshore rock just above the level of the tide, an easy ramp for a prospecting otter to pause on. You know from old stillnesses that it is a perfect otter place.

So you wait for the next resurfacing, the next eel. You wonder just how many eels are coursing through the Sound right now, given how easily the otter is catching them. Then the curved body, the raised tail, the dive. You move quickly, you sit, you still. In ten more minutes, the otter dives within a few feet of the uncovered rock and emerges almost at once on the rock. This time, there is no eel.

Oblivious to your hunched stillness on the shore, the otter begins to do otter things. It scents around the rock; it spraints; it squirms on its back, shakes the water from its fur; scratches its chin, its head, its belly; scents the air; stares at your shape in a vacant kind of way while you stare back in a marvelling kind of way.

3

You may take your pictures, you may stare through binoculars, but best of all is that you relish your own part in the situation you have achieved, your stillness that has permitted the otter to treat you like a part of its landscape.

The otter gives you five minutes of magical co-operation, five minutes that will last you a lifetime, then something it senses that you don't changes its demeanour: it barks a hoarse, soft monosyllable – "*haah!*" – and slips back into the sea-surge. On the rock it has just vacated, the otter has left messages for others of its tribe. These say that it was here, it was alone, it was safe, it was relaxed and it took its time.

The tide, you notice, is still on the rise, and your feet are wet.

◎ ◎ ◎

OTTER

They say there is an otter territory for every mile of the Skye coast. I don't disagree, although I doubt if anyone has ever checked every mile of the Skye coast to be certain. I know quite a few miles of Skye coast, some intimately, and these are where I would go to see otters. All you have to do then is give it time and stillness. And ideally you want an onshore wind that takes your scent away from a shore-bound otter (and you hope that the otter isn't coming from behind you *towards* the sea from the land!). A falling tide is often better than a rising one, but if the habitat is right and the food is plentiful, you can see otters at any state of the tide, and any state of the sea from flat calm to storm. Early in the day and late in the day, first light and last light, tip the odds in your favour, but you can also get lucky in midday sunlight.

And better by far than examining every mile of the Skye coast is to get to know a single mile inside out, upside down and backwards. And blindfolded. That is how you learn the preferences of the local otters: when they like to hunt, and where they like to come ashore, where they lie up, where the bitch has her holt, what the dog requires in the way of territory, how to tell them apart and how to tell them from interloper otters. Armed with such knowledge you can settle down, make yourself comfortable (a relative term on most Hebridean rock shores), and wait for the otter to come to you. Then you are in a position of strength, and the otter can treat you as a piece of its landscape. For example:

It is the end of a night made sleepless by a full moon in the window that lures me from my shoreline base at 3.30 in the morning, the still air scythed open by the cries of curlew and the rasps of heron. I follow an old familiar path to an old familiar rock, and there I sit and prepare to wait and get cold. The moon vanishes behind mainland mountains and the morning darkens at once, even as it begins to turn towards dawn. Sea and island are quiet, but some of the island's birds are roused – curlew and heron again and again, oystercatchers are pretty well non-stop, redshank and ringed plover add their grace notes. The mainland is a black shroud.

OTTER

Then there is a new pattern on the sea, just offshore. At the head of it is the blunt thrust of an otter muzzle from which a vee-shaped wedge spills quietly, its edges and ripples picked out in low light. A big dog otter frequents this shore. I have seen him often. A ginger muffler about his neck and jowls tempers his sleek and powerful profile with a clown's face. But then any adult otter is a captivating cocktail of missile and clown. I don't know if this is the same animal; I can't tell in this light. But he is fishing, and he may be coming my way. Then he vanishes.

In half an hour he is back in exactly the same place. He passes like a floating log travelling at the speed of the current, but then he curves back towards the very rock where I sit, and he does not stop until he has one forefoot on it, and his muzzle is testing the air not fifteen feet away. He has come to inspect my shape on his shore. Then with a single movement he flows from rock into water and leaves me a parcel of bubbles for a parting gift. And now I know he knows I am here, and what I am.

Instinct kicks in now. It tells me I have reached the wildest part of the shore in the dark, and I will be in place when daylight comes, a fragment of the landscape. Sit still, wait, watch what happens.

If you can be still and allow nature to come to you, that is when she confides in you. Quite suddenly nature comes to me in the shape of the otter, lying on his back in the water and eating an eel. This time the script is different. He dives suddenly, unexpectedly, and I am sure he discards the eel half-eaten as he dives, letting it slide away into the depths.

Why would he do that? He resurfaces almost at once and his jaws are clamped around a huge crab. That's why.

But he cannot eat the crab the way he eats an eel, and my time has come. The otter needs a shoreline rock. He chooses mine. It's the same one he chose the last time, the one he chose a thousand times before the last time. He swims towards me, crab first. One pincer flails out of the water.

He climbs onto the rock, drops the crab, looks round. I hear the crab hit the rock. I hear his teeth take hold of it. I hear the shell crack and I see it splinter. I hear his teeth crunch and grind. I see a small, brittle rain of crab shell fall onto the rock and the water. Then he appears to notice me again, and he forms a question:

"*Haah?*"

I copy the sound:

"*Haah?*"

He's puzzled:

"*Haaaaaaaahh?*"

"*Haah?*"

He takes a pace up the rock and issues a much more authoritative statement – "*Hah!*" – like that, as short and emphatic as a spit. Then, having made his point, he simply turns his back on me, and the crab flakes start to fall again. Occasionally he looks over a shoulder. In ten minutes, he has reduced the crab to shell sand. He steps off, makes no sound, leaves me a new parcel of bubbles...

☉ ☉ ☉

I rarely buy souvenirs when I travel to the edge of the land. But I do pick up stones from the shore. A well-chosen stone can reinforce and sustain connections with its landscape, and connections with landscape are the raw stuff that underpin my writing life. Right now, in the room where I write there is a stone on which the grey patina has worn away to leave the white shape of a walking polar bear. I found it at St Ninian's Cave in Galloway, which is not renowned for its polar bears but is renowned for the found art that adorns the teeming stones beneath your feet as you walk out to the saint's cave.

A second stone in that room is a dark red lump of east coast sandstone, and it too has a startling image worn into one face – a howling wolf among trees, all of it cast in eerie, creamy white. It came from a shore between the firths of Tay and Forth, where there is no wolf tradition at all, but the east coast is my native shore, Scotland's unsung shore, so what better to sing its praises than wolfsong?

But there is a third stone, and I picked it up just a few miles down the coast from where I have perched by the Sound of Sleat, on a beach by a chain of small islands that begins where an alder-fringed mountain burn empties its sweetness into Atlantic salt, and ends with a lighthouse. The place is called Sandaig. It is better known to millions of Gavin Maxwell's readers as Camusfearna, the Bay of the Alders, the setting of *Ring of Bright Water*. This third stone has no pattern on it. It is pale grey quartz, and smooth, and it sits on a bookshelf in front of a row of books by Gavin Maxwell. It is handled much more often than the other stones. It is cold to the touch. It sits up naturally and unsupported on its flat "bottom", and the face that is turned towards me has writing on it. It says:

EDAL
"Whatever joy
you had from her
give back
to Nature" GM

Edal was one of the *Ring of Bright Water* otters, and she died in the fire that destroyed Sandaig.

The words are from the dedication page of *Raven Seek Thy Brother*, the third book of what would become known as the Camusfearna trilogy. It was some time after I brought the stone home that I thought of writing that little memorial on the stone, and every now and then I go over the letters, reinforcing their message. As a link to a landscape, its power is its simplicity. I treat its message as a kind of perpetual command.

TWO

IT WILL NOT SURPRISE YOU to know, then, that one of the things I love best about islands is to go beachcombing. For otters.

There is a shore on the west coast of Mull stuffed full of that species of broad-leaved wrack that turns every other wave and ripple into ottery false alarms. I know this shore of old, know that otters live here, know the chances are that I will have it to myself, know that with the wind in the right direction and a falling tide the otter prospects will be good: time to go beachcombing. Sure enough, I found fresh spraint on a low, flat-topped rock decorated with the debris of fresh crab. But an hour and a half later there was still no trace of the diner. Beachcombing for otters is an inexact science.

I found instead a buzzard walking in a shoreline field, sometimes standing quite still, sometimes running on stiff legs like a coot, but mostly walking, and, as far as I could see, mostly failing to catch whatever it is that occupies a walking-running-standing buzzard for an hour at time – beetles, worms, voles, mice, frogs?

I also found a washed-up tree trunk, branchless and worn round and smooth by its sea voyage, and either cut into a straight length or felled that way. A mast? An escapee from a cargo of timber? An ocean traveller from, say, Nova Scotia? Or an inshore trundler from Lochaline? It was in two pieces, one beside the other. How and when did it part company with itself? Did it snap with a scream in a storm or rot apart at some frailty in the wood with one last groan?

I found a blue plastic fishbox. I prefer the old wooden ones that could kindle a driftwood fire or make a picnic table or bothy furniture. The blue box said "Ardglass and Portavogie" on the side. Where the hell is Portavogie?

But eventually, after two or three hours, I found

amid the suck and blow of slow, shallow waves beneath the listless, whispering seaweed, a furrow that was surely too straight to be the work of a conspiracy of sea and wrack and rock. But it was not an otter. It was two otters, swimming so deliberately nose-to-tail and straight as a washed-up log from Nova Scotia that it took the assistance of good binoculars to determine what was going on.

I was sitting on the low ledge of a small cliff, and ready to move nearer the water's edge as soon as the otters dived, but they did not dive. Instead, the leading otter turned at right angles towards the very shore where I sat. So I froze and the two otters nose-to-tailed straight towards me. The ringleader otter kept uttering that familiar, hoarse, interrogative "*haah?*", that back-of-the-throat monosyllable. I like to think it asks at least three questions: who are you, what are you, and what are you up to?

Both otters reached the shallows, stood up on hind legs, then barked that same question again in perfect unison. When I failed to respond with sound or gesture, one of the otters either lost its nerve or lost interest in the turn of events, executed a neat backflip and rolled away into deep water and vanished.

But the first otter still stood its ground, still stood erect, and said "*haah*?" every few seconds. I have met this phenomenon before. Not least on that early-morning Skye shoreline. By copying the sound, I have – very occasionally – participated in a protracted conversation several minutes long without having the slightest idea what kind of message either party was communicating. Mostly, nature ignores this kind of mimicry, but again very occasionally, it lures the creature closer. For the tribe of mustelids in particular, curiosity is part of their workaday lives.

Otter and I were still locked in an impasse when the second otter reappeared. It was a fabulously built, thick-set dog otter, and at once he began swimming and stomping hugely all around the bitch. It seemed to me that he was trying to lure her away from her obsessive interest in this shore-line intruder, which was clearly not an otter. He barrel-rolled in the water, which seemed to impress me more than it did her, for she turned on him in

a lithe and leathery swirl, snapped her jaws alarm-
ingly close to his muzzle, turned in less than her
own length, and at once she was standing again
– and out of the water now – and challenging me
again with another breathy bark.

"*Haah?*"

Again and again the dog otter lured her into the
water, and again and again she toyed with him or
snapped at him and returned to stand and stare
at me. Once, she uncoiled back into the water
through wrack and rock and dived through whirl-
pools of her own making. In the flowing of the
two otters, the surge and retreat of water, and the
restless heave of the seaweed, nature contrived
a kind of mobile jigsaw puzzle in which all the
pieces constantly moved yet none was ever out of
place, the puzzle never incomplete. This kind of
interaction with nature has given me some of the
most precious moments of my life. But I love it
most when it happens on nature's terms. I have
never subscribed to the notion of luring animals
into a situation that requires them to perform for
a human audience. Many people – naturalists,

writers, photographers, whatever – can achieve spectacular results with a lure of some kind or another. I don't decry it. But it's not for me.

The bitch was back, pausing again on her hind legs. It seemed she had chosen to include me in whatever fascination was occupying her mind. Then she started to turn my mimicry of her voice into what I can only describe as a game. Whenever she returned to the shore, she stood and uttered that same familiar sound:

"Haah?"

If I did not respond at once, she would repeat it and go on repeating it until I did respond, at which point she whirled round and dived into the waves again. Then she added a new twist. She squirmed along a rock ledge just above the sea and vanished where the ledge turned behind the rock. Her tail was the last of her to vanish. Seconds later her head reappeared where her tail had just been, and with the rest of her body still hidden, she barked at me again. I responded. She reversed out of sight. Then she inched forward again and peered round the rock.

"*Haah*?" she said again.

I sat motionless, suppressing the instinct to giggle, and to run and hide myself. Whether or not she became bored by my stillness, or whether she had simply reached her natural boredom threshold, I have no way of knowing. I have often thought since then that I should have tried to hide too, to see if she responded differently, but stillness is what brought her to me in the first place, and I suppose I reasoned at the time that any movement would have ended the thing before she wanted it to. Anyway, she got bored.

She leaped off her rock, and in my mind as I write this is an image of her frozen in mid-air, all four legs splayed wide, her tail straight out, her jaws wide open. And in that attitude she thudded into the water with an enormous splash, and the two otters rolled away from the chaos.

The next I saw of them they were a hundred yards away, swimming companionably north. I wonder what it is that otters do when they swim off in tandem knowing they have hopelessly beguiled a human bystander. Or perhaps they knew no aftermath and they were already preoccupied with the day's next adventure. Perhaps the only aftermath is mine, and that will last a lifetime for this beguiled island wanderer who loves nothing better than to go beachcombing for otters.

Gavin Maxwell wrote in *Ring of Bright Water*:

There is a perpetual mystery and excitement in living on the seashore, which is in part a return to childhood and in part because for all of us the sea's edge remains the edge of the unknown; the child sees the bright shells, the vivid weeds and red sea-anemones of the rock pools with wonder and with the child's eye for minutiae; the adult who retains wonder brings to his gaze some partial knowledge which can but increase it, and he brings, too, the eye of association and of symbolism, so that at the edge of the ocean he stands at the brink of his own unconscious.

Sitting at the edge of the ocean, I suddenly wanted to drink to that. Where's my hipflask?

THREE

Not all otters are thirled to Hebridean shore-lines. In the heart of what I think of as my writer's home territory around the first mountains above the southern edge of the Highlands, there is a watershed where I walk often. A lochan lies there beneath wooded hills, and shines like a brooch on a crumpled cloak of glacial moraine and old oakwood. On a May morning, with the sun newly roused, it is a place packed with nature's possibilities.

Better than a brooch is the notion of the lochan as an eye, the landscape's watcher, commanding miles of high country. But I think of it in that way only because Henry David Thoreau taught me to. The grandfather of America's admirable nature writing tradition wrote in *Walden*:

ENCOUNTERS IN THE WILD

A lake is the landscape's most beautiful and expressive feature. It is earth's eye, looking into which the beholder measures the depth of his own nature.

It is one of those mind-blowing original thoughts that changed forever the way I look at a watersheet, and it is not a million miles away from Maxwell's "at the edge of the ocean he stands on the brink of his own unconscious". Over the years that I have been accustomed to walking up to the lochan in every season and at every hour of the day (and a few of the night), I have acquired a good measure of the depth of my own nature.

The otter's nature there, however, has proved more elusive. Unlike the otter of the islands, which is unfazed by daylight, in the landlocked heartlands of the watershed the otter is mostly a haunter of dusk and dawn and the hours in between. I know where it comes from and where it goes, for it advertises its travels as legibly as a spread map. It climbs like so up from the burn (which it has followed upstream from the river half a mile away), squirts through the mesh of the stock fence (see its flattened, narrow trail through the tussocks), contours across the rough ground to a crossroads with a fox-roe-deer-pine-marten path where it pauses to spraint, and from there drops down a short, steep ramp to the south shore of the lochan. There it skirts a big rock dumped by an old glacier and a favourite feeding perch for buzzards, owls, merlins, kestrels. And a wandering sea eagle roosted for a week over there in that rambling old oak on the steepest slope of the east bank. It littered the ground beneath the tree with pellets the size of my fist.

There is another sprainting place at the edge of the water, just beyond a perfectly formed grass-walled-and-roofed tunnel one otter wide and a yard long. I have an unfulfilled ambition to see the otter negotiate that tunnel.

In winter, snow consolidates the tunnel even more, and the ramp becomes one of several otter slides around the watershed. And when the snow lies on the frozen surface of the water, footprints confirm the otter's preferred route across to the far side where it hauls out by a narrow outflow. Here it spraints again on the bank before squirming down the outflow (more occasional spraints on a rock in mid-stream), which feeds into a second smaller and more overgrown lochan, which in turn seeps away into a reedbed where the otter finally covers its tracks and heads for God-knows-where.

It seems to avoid the lochan on its return journey, in preference, I suspect, for a longer meander back down the burn to the river in the south. In the snow, or in occasional patches of wet mud near the lochan, all the footprints head north, but in the sandy curves of the burn they head both north and south. There is so much to read about the otter, then, but despite many, many hours at the lochan and more following my idea of the otter's regular route, I have never seen one there.

But I see them on the river, especially in its quieter floodplain stretches. Here is a level stretch of bank, topped by a mile of trees – alders, willow and birch mostly. The slow, gnawing river toys with the roots. A wide and shallow heap of sediment below the bank is laced every morning with the five-toed, webbed, overnight tracks of otters. I used to live here. Early and late, I walked that mile of bank. On an early morning of early March I saw the bitch imprinting the frosted grass. Her spoor was indistinct footprints, a distinct furrow left by her trailing tail. She shouldered aside a ground mist. Her side-on shape was long and low and slender. She moved with purpose on short legs along the top of the bank. In profile, her head was long and narrow. She was dark grey-brown, and her fur was wet (it dries to a paler, gingery shade). She was off-white under her chin and down her breast…her identity card.

She stopped without warning, turned her head left to stare across the river, to stare at me where I was leaning against a tree. Now her head and muzzle were wide, her ears tiny and set high, and her brown eyes stared. She knew me, or rather she was familiar with my scent, my shape, my presence. From nose to tail-tip she was perhaps a yard and a half long. Her mate, the dog otter, was a foot longer and heftier. He wore a forehead scar. He'd been around. He wore no white under his chin or down his front. Much of the time, he kept his distance.

She still stared, one forepaw raised. Then she walked on, curved tightly down to her left, descended the bank on a path of bare earth, her path. At the foot of it was a sprawl of tree roots. Something, some signal, moved between her and the roots, for two cubs about half her size emerged to meet her. One had a white front and one did not. If there was a greeting, I did not hear it. There was no fuss. They eased into the water as if the river was waiting for them. The water was their true home. The bitch dived, blew bubbles; the cubs swam after her on the surface. The mist closed in behind them.

I know otters occasionally travel up to the lochan at least two at a time because sometimes in past winters the snow showed two sets of meandering tracks on the frozen surface, and one set was bigger than the other. And I want to know if it was the dog and the bitch, or the bitch with a well-grown cub or cubs, or two well-grown cubs exploring independently, or something else I haven't thought of.

Why do I want to know these things? Two reasons. One is simply to write them down, for my trade is that of a writer and I wander the wild places of the land in search of their secrets to try and write them down. The second reason is more complicated. It has to do with Thoreau's observation about the beholder measuring the depths of his own nature.

I do a lot of beholding. There is no better time to behold than a May morning or evening, when it seems as if all nature's tribes are on the move at once and giving voice, and the earlier the morning or the later the evening, the more accessible are their secrets. As Seton Gordon put it: "…the spirit of the high and lonely places revealed herself…"

Writing down the spirit of the high and lonely places, then, is a kind of *cause célèbre* for me, and I believe that such an abstract idea is more tangible in places where my relationship with nature is an intimate one, those places where I am inclined to go again and again over years, and so acquire a sense of the prevailing patterns of nature at work.

Mostly, such places are inside my core territory. I have had heart-stopping moments that will live with me forever in a handful of other countries – Alaska, Iceland, Norway, Switzerland – and I am often on the move across Scotland. I have met otters on many of our islands, and found their tracks in the snow at 3,000 feet in the Cairngorms. But most of these have been primarily moments of spectacle. Moments of *understanding*, however, are more elusive unless I am so familiar with a particular set of nature's circumstances that what I behold is an element of a recurring pattern. Everything I gather from familiar landscapes is more precious as a beholder, as a nature writer, because my own constant presence in that land-scape is also a part of the pattern, and I reclaim the ancient right of my own species to be part of nature myself.

So I walk up to the watershed on a May morning. An otter has been there not long before me, for a sprint by the rock is wet and glistening and dew-fresh. Is the otter still here? Using the lie of the land I can make a circuit of the lochan

without showing myself to anything on the surface
or the banks, and climb up to a rock twenty or
thirty feet above the water and settle there with
a view over the lochan and the moraines and the
forest to near and distant hills.

Over two hours I will see these: the nesting pair
of Canada geese (a direct link with Thoreau: he
mentions them specifically in *Walden*), a heron that
drifts in from the south and works the shore and
the shallows from the shadow of what I now think
of as the sea eagle's oak, a water vole (the first I've
seen here), three different male little grebes (I know
the three messy nest sites hidden in shoreline vegetation), a great-spotted woodpecker (flying in long,
shallow, airy bounces), a male cuckoo (calling on a
wire), a roebuck (barking in a stand of willows), two
mute swans in flight and heading north (has the
resident cob on the nearby loch driven them out?),
an osprey with a fish for a lowered undercarriage
(his nest is on a dead birch trunk left standing in an
area of clear-felled forestry), skylarks, tree pipits,
a male redstart, reed buntings, a sun-burnished
red fox (nosing along an old drystane dyke), and

the resident male buzzard (restlessly quartering his territory, and he can measure the depths of his own nature by beholding the lochan from directly overhead). If the otter is still here, it doesn't show. After two hours by the high rock, I leave discreetly for a late breakfast. My mind is buoyant with the sensations and encounters of nature's morning, but the otter has left a small and familiar taste of disappointment – one more near miss. I will be back at the rock in the late evening. Such is the nature of the beholder on the watershed.

FOUR

SHETLAND AND I GOT ON WELL together from the first moment of the first day. There is the singular charm of island light, there is a further embellishment of northern light, and then there is the light of northern islands, which unites the two and elevates the results into something like light as a state of grace. Why wouldn't there be otters here?

The Shetland that I came to know best is the island of Yell, right in the middle of the archipelago. In particular, there was an early April week in a tiny caravan a few yards above the high tide at Mid Yell Voe, where every day I lingered over long and lazy evening meals watching otters and eider ducks from the window by the table.

Wherever you look seaward from Yell, and especially if you have acquired a little bit of height, the views in every direction are of other islands and their intervening scraps of ocean and sounds, and the interplay of sunlight and shadow and wind and rain and rainbows. At dawns and dusks of late May and June, the pageant of natural light on so much fractured land and ocean is symphonic, and nightfall is little more than an hour of gloaming.

The corner of Yell I recall most fondly is called Ness of Galtagarth. We met for the first time one cold and sunlit morning of that early April week. It is a small, flat and infertile island, umbilically linked to Yell by a tombolo. Its outer shore is a treachery of rounded and knife-edged boulders liberally coated with seaweed, all of which spills seawards from an eroding peat bank. The peat, where it encounters the rock, overhangs or crumbles into a more-or-less continuous alleyway the width of one otter.

Shetland is a benevolent host to otters. There are hundreds of miles of untrampled coastline and a sea as liberally stuffed with fish as any otter could dream of. In all the waters of the British Isles, Shetland is something of a stronghold. It was here in 1983 that wildlife cameraman Hugh Miles broke new ground with a remarkable television film called *The Track of the Wild Otter*. At the time, I was a newspaper journalist nurturing dreams of writing about nature for a living. That film was an electrifying jolt to my ambitions. It was – and it remains – a high-water mark in wildlife film-making, a work of rare insight and creative beauty.

I set out to wander round the entire coast of that wee island. Half an hour later, I saw my first otter. It was fifty yards out and swimming parallel to the shore, and deploying that purposeful porpoising technique of an otter on the march. For as long as the otter's direction of travel and the essentially curved nature of the shore permitted, I kept pace with it, running and scrambling (and falling) while it was underwater, crouching and freezing when it surfaced. Only the otter was dignified in its move-ments. I was trying perhaps just a little too hard to keep the otter in sight as the shore curved away from its line of travel, instead of paying attention to where I was, to where I was putting my feet, and to learning something of the lie of the land and its otter-watching possibilities. As a result, I failed to see what I should have seen, and so squandered what may well be the best opportunity to watch an otter at very close quarters that I will ever know.

Even as the swimming otter disappeared from view, I became suddenly and woefully belatedly aware of a second otter. It was a large, gingery dog otter, curled up and dozing in the sun perhaps five paces away from me. In the same moment that I registered the rhythmical rise and fall of his flank while trying to come to terms with nature's gift of such an opportunity, the overhanging edge of the peat bank gave way beneath my left boot. The disturbance was not loud, but it didn't have to be to gatecrash the cordons of an otter's mid-morning doze. He took the twenty yards of shoreline rocks at a flat-out blur, dived without pause into the water, surfaced twenty yards further out, and only from that sanctuary did he turn and scrutinise me in what I imagine was silent outrage. Then he dived again and did not resurface in my sight. I considered his sprint across the rocks, and the nature of the terrain he had just covered with such sure-footed ease. I equated it to me covering a hundred metres of Skye's Cuillin Ridge in ten seconds, from a sleeping start.

I walked on along the shore, and at a more considered pace, stopping often to examine a great deal of evidence of otter presence, but I had ridden my luck with the otters themselves and I saw no more that morning. Instead there was a pair of whimbrels that shrieked dryly at me and stepped up from the shingle into the air, and hung there like coat hangers for a moment, before wheeling away across the voe. The wind dropped as I walked and sunlight burned fiercely through a few midday hours. The next day I had to leave Yell and it snowed, otter tracks in white at the edge of the ocean.

FIVE

THE RIVER EARN, Perthshire, emerges fully formed
from the east end of Loch Earn at the village of St
Fillans. One gloomy, damp and windless noontide
of mid-October, the day has infused my mood,
and I imagine I would make poor company. But
in any case, I almost always work alone. The
aura of gloom is further enhanced by the press
of trees about the banks (even on the sunniest of
days there is more shadow than sunlight on this
particular stretch of the river); by the relentless,
wearying smirr that has been falling since dawn,
drenching every particle and molecule of land
and air; and by the equally incessant roaring of
red deer stags unseen on cloud-shrouded hillsides
to north and south, a sound that falls about my
ears like the battle cries of armies from the Dark
Ages. On such a day, the most resolute watcher of

nature's moods is apt to find his resolve demateri-
alise into a mulch of cold porridge. So what the
hell am I doing here?

I have noticed over the last few years that the
local beavers (whose signatures are indelibly
incised everywhere among the wooded banks)
rather seem to enjoy such days. The textbooks will
tell you that they are creatures of the dawn and
the dusk, and mostly the textbooks are right. But
they also mostly fail to mention that a noontide
like this one could almost be mistaken for dawn
or dusk, and that in such circumstances, beavers
behave as if it *were* dawn or dusk. The gloom
renders them almost invisible, for they are the
same grey shade as the day itself, and besides, it
also discourages human presence. So the beavers
can be up and doing in the middle of the day, safe
from all sources of daylight disturbance, right?

Not quite.

I have known the River Earn for many years.
It flows east to join the Tay east of Perth, and
the Tay has coursed through my entire life. I
grew up on its banks and it is forever pulling me

home again from every corner of Scotland and beyond. So I was thrilled when beavers colonised this stretch of the Earn very early in the story of their reintroductions (both planned and "accidental") into Scotland, and I got to know it particularly well when I was researching a book on the subject called *Nature's Architect* (Saraband, 2015). I have followed their progress here ever since. But I had never thought of it as an otter river before, and while that does not mean there were no otters here, it does mean that if they were around it was as a more-or-less wholly nocturnal presence. Then beavers moved in, then they began to make the changes that beavers like to make to a landscape, and then I began seeing otters. Otters like the presence of beavers, and seem to seek it out.

This intrigues me. In Scotland, otters had not lived alongside beavers for 400 years before this twenty-first-century reintroduction began. Yet it has taken them no time at all to reconvene their historic relationship. This suggests that race memory is indestructible, that the race of otters has always known there are advantages to be gained from being around the race of beavers. It is true in North America, it is true in Western Europe, and in Scotland the two species have simply taken up where they left off, centuries before.

All of which helps to explain why, one October noontide on the River Earn with the day's smothering greyness contriving to dampen even the tempestuous shades of oak and birch and willow and alder in their autumn prime, I was watching with some fascination what looked at first glance like a stash of fallen leaves over by the far bank. I knew from repeated visits to this same stretch of river that these particular leaves were new additions to the local beaver architecture. There were two things about the leaves that made them worth a second glance and then a long, lingering stare. One was when I realised they were not fallen leaves at all, but rather harvested leaves – beaver-harvested leaves. An inspection with binoculars revealed that their stems were still attached to long, skinny twigs of a more-or-less uniform length, and I also knew that they had been piled against a slowly subsiding remnant of what had been a small beaver dam. The other thing about them was there had just been an unusual movement at the heart of the stash: it had just heaved upwards then subsided again.

I decided the only rational explanation was that a beaver was at work just below it. I also suspected that the dam had originally provided tranquil water behind it for an underwater entrance to a burrowed bank-side lodge, which would be the preferred accommodation on such a turbulent river where a timber-built lodge could succumb easily to frequent spates. It was possible that the slowly decomposing and submerging dam still provided that service and that even now the beaver was moving the strips of leaves into its larder in the lodge.

It struck me then that only five years ago I had never seen a wild beaver, but now – such is the fascination of my job – I could examine a pile of leaves and interpret its purpose in some detail. It may have been the middle of the day, but as the leaves heaved again, I fully expected a beaver to slip into view at any moment. No sooner had the thought formed than the pile of leaves burst apart, the spectacle given added impact because it was almost silent. Long stems of autumn leaves were hurled in every direction, so that it looked for a few moments as if the air was strewn with madly waving prayer flags, then the source of the explosion powered through the chaos at a steep upward trajectory until it was almost completely out of the water, and only when it curved back towards the surface of the water in a monumental splashdown did the soundtrack catch up with the spectacle.

When the mayhem subsided, an otter was swimming in a wide midstream arc among tumbling leaves, an arc that first led it away from the splash landing and then back towards the now widely scattered leaves. But almost at once – and in complete silence and with barely a ripple – a beaver materialised on the surface and began edging back and forward, upstream and downstream, a patrolling sentry intent on denying the otter a second opportunity to inflict whatever turmoil it had just visited on the beavers' underworld before it had been discouraged with such dramatic effect. The hostility and the tension between the two animals was unmistakable. For the next minute, they confronted each other without making contact, without giving way, and with nothing but the sound of the river to work with. A prelude to further hostilities? Or a necessary striking of postures so that neither lost face before they went about their business?

The quiet was shattered by the bellow of a stag, much closer and therefore lower down the hill than anything I had heard that morning. Neither otter nor beaver reacted to the sound. But in my mind's eye, I saw the red deer stag and a challenging rival strut through the preliminary ritual known as parallel walking, in which they size each other up before locking antlers and putting each other to the ultimate test. What was going on in the water had an element of that ritual of stand-off and appraisal, and I wondered where else in the wild world could I participate simply through my dead-still presence in the simultaneous and tension-laden moments of three such diverse creatures as otter, beaver and stag.

The impasse on the river was resolved by the beaver in the most prosaic way imaginable. It simply turned its back on the otter and began retrieving what it could of the leaves and ferrying them back to the disordered remnants of the original pile. The otter's response was the one that took me by surprise, for it crossed the river to my side, and left the water by a track through trees and thick undergrowth that I had noticed before, but which I had assumed was a beaver track. (In truth, there is no reason why they would not both use it, and quite possibly they also share it with badger and fox and deer coming to the water to drink.)

At the top of the bank, the otter paused with one forepaw raised, and looked back over its shoulder to where the beaver was still gathering and reordering the scattered foliage, swimming downstream and collecting it in substantial mouthfuls as it turned back into the current. Back at the site of the original stash, it piled the recovered stems against the quiet side of the dam, so that they were out of the current and formed a compact raft, the bottom of which may even have been resting on part of the dam itself. Then it swam back out into the open river, and began patrolling the outer edge of the dam again while the otter still watched. The otter may have seen this manoeuvre as a new challenge, because it turned and retraced its steps down to the water's edge, where it paused again. The beaver met this gesture by swimming straight towards the otter, turning in its own length a few yards from the bank, then smashing its leathery paddle-shaped tail onto the surface and disappearing in the same instant.

The otter, which must have seen such beaver indignation before, did not react at all. Then it turned back up the track and walked away upstream, but along the top of the bank, keeping a certain distance between itself and the river – the required discretion that is the better part of valour.

◉ ◉ ◉

I have witnessed two other sulky stand-offs before, but this was my high-water mark of otter-beaver interaction. Mostly they seem to put up with each other because they have no choice, and because out-and-out hostilities are not in the interests of either of them, given that both are formidably well armed with teeth and powerful jaws. But only the otters stand to gain from the relationship. As far as I can see, the beaver gains nothing at all from proximity to otters.

The beaver is a vegetarian, and the otter is a carnivore. Newly emerged beaver kitts are certainly vulnerable to otters, and otters can get inside a beaver lodge the same way that a beaver does, and it seems to me that tension between the two species is highest when there are new kitts around. There is obviously no corresponding threat from beavers to otter cubs.

The other bonus for otters is that they like what beavers do, the way they manipulate water. For example, on the Earn the beavers dug out a canal parallel to the river, a canal which the river replenishes whenever the water level rises. The beavers also partially dammed the downstream end of the canal and dug out a deep pool there. Fish, especially young fish, love the canal and the pool, and I have seen a few larger fish resting up in there too, so it is hardly surprising that canal and pool are regularly visited by otters.

But in addition to the prospect of easy fishing in the pool, it also indulges the otters' capacity for play. The river and its wood are full of otter toys – pine cones, sprigs of rowan berries, bones, fishermen's floats, the occasional ball that comes downstream in spates having been washed from upstream gardens...all these have ended up in otter jaws and otter hands here, to be thrown, pounced upon, or dragged to the bottom of the pool to be released so that they rise to the surface, only to find the otter is already there to catch them. I am looking forward to a snowy winter: I would put money on the otter making a slide from the top of the bank to the pool, and I want to be there when it opens for business.

◉ ◉ ◉

The solitary otter with a found object for a "toy" is as captivating a spectacle for the watcher as it is for the otter. But when a slide is involved, more than just the game changes.

"We find the animals going through much the same stages as we do," wrote the American author Ernest Thompson Seton a little over a hundred years ago in his book, *Wild Animals at Home*. "First, the struggle for food, then for mates, and later, when they have no cause to worry about either, they seek for entertainment. Quite a number of our animals have invented amusements. Usually these are mere games of tag, catch, or tussle, but some have gone farther and have a regular institution, with a set place to meet, and apparatus provided. This is the highest form of all, and one of the best illustrations of it is found in the jovial Otter…probably every individual of the species frequents some Otter slide. This is any convenient steep hill or bank, sloping down into deep water, prepared by much use, and worn into a smooth shoot that becomes especially serviceable when snow or ice are there to act as lightning lubricants."

This game is as old as otters. One such bank graced a hill burn that flowed into the River Dochart a little to the east of Loch Dochart. I got to know it when I lived just a couple of miles along Glen Dochart for a few years. The bank curved above a right-angled bend in the burn, an all-but-vertical twenty-feet-high wall of sparse vegetation and bare mud, topped by an overhanging frieze of hill grass and heather. It had the look of impermanence about it, as if one hefty spate would undermine the whole edifice and topple it into the burn. The hoarse song of a waterfall hidden beyond an upstream buttress was the insistent voice of the place, and the succession of rocky steps and larger boulders the burn must negotiate between buttress and bend provided an elaborate array of grace notes, beyond which the burn fuelled and deepened the wide pool at the base of the bank. That pool was the inevitable prerequisite for the otter's slide game, and bisecting the bank from top to bottom was the shallow groove of the slide.

It was quite bare, worn into that "smooth shoot", in Seton's phrase (somehow so much more

visually expressive than the English "chute"), by
the passage of God knows how many otter under-
bellies. The fact that the otters were invariably
wet when they used it, instantly slicked the surface
to a slippery sheen even in the driest of weather.
But as Seton suggested, snow or ice – or ideally
both – transformed the game and gave it a manic,
competitive edge.

They took the slide head-first, some slid off the
end into the water with admirable grace, some
contrived an acrobatic leap to create a spectacular
splash. But every otter swam immediately for the
same corner of the pool, hauled out, and sprinted
back up to the top of the bank to slide again.
Bigger animals barged the smaller ones aside.
Occasionally, one otter might try to gain advan-
tage by cramponing back up the slide, but almost
invariably the strategy was foiled by another otter
coming down. A collision was avoided only if the
uphill otter gave up the climb and slid backwards
into the pool.

Twice, I saw four otters at the slide, but sometimes the quantity of tracks and droppings

suggested a larger gathering had been at play, and I had the feeling that otters travelled to the slide from both upstream and downstream territories, that it was a place where territorial hostilities were suspended. The unrestrained nature of the play appeared to thrive on its collaborative quality. Seton described it perfectly, a place where otters met, with apparatus provided. But five or six years after I stumbled on the place, a ferocious flash flood hit the area and the bank and its slide collapsed, realigning the burn in the process.

If the otters ever built a new slide somewhere else in the glen, I never found it.

AFTERWORD

THE OTTER (*Lutra lutra*) is a mustelid, a family of carnivorous mammals that includes weasels, stoats, badgers and pine martens. There are thirteen different otter species worldwide. Ours is the Eurasian otter, and it is widely distributed throughout Europe.

The UK population has recovered well in the twenty-first century after a long and disastrous decline, and although Scotland is still its strong-hold with somewhere between 8,000 and 10,000 animals, it is once again in every English county too. In those years of recovery, it has reclaimed much of its historical territory and can now be found almost anywhere between Shetland and the south coast, wherever there is suitable habitat. In Scotland, more than half the population is on the Atlantic coast and the islands of the west and north. In fresh water, the otter inhabits rivers, burns, lochs, canals and open wetland.

There is a widespread tendency to talk about "river otters" and "sea otters" as if they were two different species, but they are one and the same, and they can – and do – flow seamlessly between the two habitats, and cope effortlessly with the different diets that implies: fish like trout, salmon and eels (and frogs and toads in springtime) in fresh water, and at sea they catch anything from crabs and lobsters to lumpsuckers and dogfish. And otters that spend their lives on sea coasts and islands routinely seek out fresh water to clean salt from their fur to maintain the efficiency of its insulation.

But the two environments may produce different behaviour. Inland, the otter is mostly nocturnal, but in the sea it is happy to be up and doing at any hour of the day or night. And there may be differences in breeding patterns too. In theory, otters can have cubs at any time, and will give birth to anything between one and four cubs. But my friend and wildlife photographer of genius, Laurie Campbell, has noticed that cubs first appear on rivers like the Tweed in late winter, whereas late summer is much more common in the Hebrides. They emerge around sixty days after birth. Otters can live for up to ten years in the wild, although the average age is probably four or five years.

Home for an otter is a holt, usually a natural cavity in a bank or shoreline, often among tree roots, sometimes in a hollow tree, or a chamber it has dug for itself in a bank, with an underwater entrance and a vertical shaft for an air vent.

They can be quite vocal, and in addition to that "*haah!*" questioning sound, they mostly use a clear, far-carrying whistle. Anger produces the occasional scream or growl.

Studies have suggested an inland otter might patrol up to twenty miles of river, but no more than three or four miles of sea coast. But generalising with otters is tricky and unreliable, and they sometimes undertake long land journeys, often crossing high watersheds.

Otter folklore is surprisingly thin on the ground, and while there are traditions in Japan and North America, the European otter's solitary claim to mythological fame seems to be a Scandinavian tradition in which it shape-shifts into a dwarf.

Literature, however, has tended to treat otters very well, and especially since the most famous otter book of all (Gavin Maxwell's *Ring of Bright Water*) was published in 1960. Single-handedly, that book transformed the relationship between people and otters, and almost overnight they metamorphosed from vermin into superstars. The book has sold several million copies and still travels the world in twenty different languages.

Ted Hughes's otter is "Four-legged yet water-gifted to outfish fish" and "Gallops along land he no longer belongs to; / Re-enters the water by melting…" And the Perthshire poet Kenneth Steven's is "Three feet of gymnastics / Taking on an ocean".

Miriam Darlington's *Otter Country* (Granta, 2012) includes this gorgeous image:

Supple as a rope made out of silk, he nuzzles his flanks and like a cat, he wriggles and rolls in the sun, then gradually coils himself into a pretzel of fur.

Compare and contrast Gavin Maxwell's image of his otter Mijbil the first time he ever watched it play in a bath: "…making enough slosh and splash for a hippo…"

Yet still, for all our adoration, ours is the only species the otter has to worry about. On the coast there is conflict around fish farms, and inland, especially on salmon rivers, there is conflict with the angling fraternity, and, despite legal protection, illegal persecution still happens. And of course, otters show very little road sense, and every year, we kill hundreds of them on our roads.

On the other hand, on a deserted single-track road on the west coast of Mull, this happened:

Late in the day, northing, the light going, crawling past an unmoving heron, I braked hard as what I thought was a cat materialised at the roadside. Where the hell did that come from? But it was not a cat, it was an otter, heading from the shore to the trees on the other side of the road. And naturally, being an otter with no road sense, it stopped in the middle and faced the car at a dozen yards. What now? After a few seconds, it astounded me by turning its back and trotting along the road. I followed in second gear, and for twenty or thirty yards I drove along Mull's main west coast road ("main" being a relative term, it was about a yard wider than my car), tailing an otter at about ten miles per hour. Then it stopped and looked round suddenly, reappraised the situation and hit the boulder-strewn shore running and disappeared into the sea.

It had been my third otter of the day, and moments later I saw my fourth. In my mind as I write is an image of that fourth otter just after it had leapt from an offshore rock; and what I see is an otter frozen in mid-air, four legs splayed wide, her tail straight out behind her, her jaws wide open. And I remembered my beachcombing hours and I thought:

"What, you again?"

My experience of otters on Mull shores has been that no encounter is less than unforgettable, and I like to think that a long apprenticeship in the company of the Mull land-and-sea-scape has a lot to do with that. Ah, but then, finally, there are the otters that no one tells you about. Three days after my four-otter day, a thousand feet up in the quietest of Mull's hill country, I was on a quest for other things, other traits of island nature, other savours of wildness – golden plover song, golden eagle shadows, that kind of thing. What I found was a flat rock thrusting out from the bank of a hill burn into the midstream, and there, as far from the sea as you can get on an island like Mull, were otter spraints. They looked like little dead snakes. They were made up from bits and pieces of little dead fish – bones in short parallel sequences, bits of scales.

That first rock was a sign, a dropped hint you might say, of what lay beyond, a message to be read by seeing eyes, but all it said was "an otter passed". Up on the watershed was the lochan that spawned the burn. Here, at the burn's outflow, were more rocks, and many more spraints, so many of them and in so many stages of texture and decomposition, so many scraps of little dead fish, that their message was unambiguous. It said: "Many otters pass, all the time!"

I began to work round the lochan. The flattened grass and heather routes of otters were everywhere. In places the spraints lay in heaps several inches high. Here was a kind of hub of the otter tribe, and it had clearly been in use for a very long time. The tracks fanned out from the lochan to every compass point. Low hills hemmed in two sides of the watershed. Otter tracks climbed the hills as well as descending the burns. One dived into a burn and into underwater holes. Then so did another one. Each diving-in place was marked, but here the spraints were tiny, nothing more than shorthand messages in the language of otters, conveying the business of otters to other otters. Alas, I don't have that kind of fluency.

From one hilltop, I looked down on the lochan 500 feet below, the slate-grey hub-cum-crossroads of an otter realm that extends in every direction and crosses three watersheds.

On the way down again, I found a golden eagle pellet, and nearby a single discarded red deer leg bone, bloody but fleshless. So up here, otter knows eagle. It has the feel of a primitive place.

Even now, comparatively few human eyes will look down on it. Mull's tourism preferences lie elsewhere. I would love to know how long otters have been coming and going from here.

For a moment, I saw it not as a simple lochan, but as a kind of crater, the centrepiece of a volcano from which issued not lava and fire, but otters and water.

JIM CRUMLEY IS A NATURE WRITER, journalist, poet, and passionate advocate for our wildlife and wild places. He is the author of more than thirty books, and is a newspaper and magazine columnist and an occasional broadcaster on both BBC radio and television. He has written companions to this volume on the barn owl, fox, swan, hare, skylark, badger and kingfisher, and there are further titles planned. He has also written in depth on topics as diverse as beavers, eagles, wolves, mountains, seasons and species reintroductions.

PUBLISHED BY Saraband

Digital World Centre, 1 Lowry Plaza
The Quays, Salford, M50 3UB

and

Suite 202, 98 Woodlands Road
Glasgow, G3 6HB

www.saraband.net

Cover illustration: © Carry Akroyd

ISBN: 9781912235049